I0014388

YOUR KNOWLEDGE HAS

Natasha Maingi

Cloud Computing

GRIN Verlag

Bibliografische Information der Deutschen Nationalbibliothek:

Die Deutsche Bibliothek verzeichnet diese Publikation in der Deutschen National-
bibliografie; detaillierte bibliografische Daten sind im Internet über http://dnb.d-
nb.de/ abrufbar.

Imprint:

Copyright © 2011 GRIN Verlag GmbH
Druck und Bindung: Books on Demand GmbH, Norderstedt Germany
ISBN: 978-3-656-59981-4

This book at GRIN:

http://www.grin.com/en/e-book/269109/cloud-computing

GRIN - Your knowledge has value

Der GRIN Verlag publiziert seit 1998 wissenschaftliche Arbeiten von Studenten, Hochschullehrern und anderen Akademikern als eBook und gedrucktes Buch. Die Verlagswebsite www.grin.com ist die ideale Plattform zur Veröffentlichung von Hausarbeiten, Abschlussarbeiten, wissenschaftlichen Aufsätzen, Dissertationen und Fachbüchern.

Visit us on the internet:

http://www.grin.com/

http://www.facebook.com/grincom

http://www.twitter.com/grin_com

Security in Cloud Computing

Introduction

Computers have increasingly become the central tool for information management for governments, corporations, non-profit organizations and individuals around the globe. The emergence of the internet has only solidified this fact even more. As computers have acquired this significant and dominant role in the affairs of mankind, a plethora and wide-array of advancements in computer technology has naturally occurred. Relatively recent hardware innovations have brought the world tablet PCs, transformer pads, smartphones with extraordinary computing capabilities, and desktop PCs with unprecedented storage and processing speeds. The realm of software development has produced countless pieces of software which cover an exceedingly wide range of functions. Even so, neither software, nor hardware alone stands as the most cutting edge computing tool. Interestingly enough, it is a marriage between the two that has become the single most ground-breaking revolution in current computing. It is known as cloud computing. Although cloud computing has various security-based disadvantages which must be addressed by cloud providers as well as consumers, the solution to these disadvantages, as well as the benefits of employing cloud computing in general, greatly outweigh the disadvantages.

While the notion of cloud computing has arguably been around as long as the idea of the internet itself, cloud computing as it is understood today got its kick start with companies such as Salesforce.com and Amazon Web Service which both offered online applications (Hempel, 2009; Tonellato, 2001). Witnessing the success of these two endeavors and seeing an opportunity for expansion in this realm, Google launched its own cloud computing service, Google Docs, in 2006 (Langley, 2008). Since then, countless other companies have entered the marketplace, each offering different kinds of cloud computing services. The benefits harvested from cloud computing has kept customers flocking and promises to keep them running towards the technology.

Cloud computing presents a host of benefits to its users. These benefits include reduced cost for software applications, reduced cost for electricity consumption, increased IT automation, increased storage capacity, and increased user mobility (Shacklett, 2011). In addition to these significant primary benefits, secondary benefits from employing cloud computing services are enjoyed by organizations around the world. Such secondary benefits include a greater focus on product or service development (by redirecting the funds saved in using cloud computing to products or services), a more flexible IT team (being that many updates and repairs are dealt with by the cloud computing service provider), a better public relations image (as the companies reduce their carbon footprint because of its large reduction in energy consumption), and a less stressful workplace environment (due to the mobility permitted by cloud computing which allows employs and organization members to access material from locations outside of the traditional place of business).

With all of these amazing primary and secondary benefits, most would see cloud computing as a panacea for information management at an organization. However, not everyone so readily jumps on the cloud computing bandwagon. In fact, numerous IT experts suggest that not only is cloud computing unsecure, its risks may in fact outweigh its benefits (Juels & Opera, 2013). While there are a few other factors which critics attack when it comes to cloud computing, the force of the attacks essentially boil down to security. In fact, it has almost become common knowledge that CIOs and IT personnel around the globe who are reluctant to employ cloud computing in their organizations cite security as the number one reason for avoiding cloud computing. Indeed, being based on the internet does suggest cloud computing services are naturally susceptible to security issues which could be utterly devastating to large companies in the event that they slipped from potentiality into reality. Moreover, the security issues are far more complex and qualitatively different from normal outsourcing issues (Owens, 2010). Understanding how cloud computing security best functions intrinsically involves first understanding the main security threats of cloud computing. The primary security risks associated with cloud computing include the chance of engaging in unsecure data transfer, the risk of employing unsecure software interfaces, and the risk of storing data in an unsecured online environment. These primary security risks branch out into more specific areas each having specific concerns associated with them.

Security Risks in Data Transfer in Cloud Computing

At its very core, cloud computing involves transferring information from provincial devices or a network to a host via the internet. On the surface, this move seems simple and relatively innocent. Nevertheless, it has the potential to unwittingly expose users' information to third parties. The weakness in data transfer from a local system to the cloud is not so much a weakness which stems from cloud computing services in general; rather it is a weakness which exists because of the medium in which communication is destined to take place between a user and a cloud computing service provider. This medium, of course, is the internet. Any information to be communicated over the internet is automatically at risk of being intercepted by unconnected, malicious third parties. Unlike local devices or intranets around which physical security systems can be installed or which otherwise are relatively easy to monitor, the internet is a vast ocean of information occupied by countless entities that in its immenseness provides no such parallel security as is enjoyed in an organization's isolated network.

Solution to Security Risks in Data Transfer in Cloud Computing

The solution to counter the inherent security risks involved in transferring data to the

cloud is employing cyber certification and encryption which can be offered by various platforms.

Platforms allowing secure transfer of information include secure file transfer protocol (SFTP),

file transfer protocol secure (FTPS), and Applicability Statement 2 (AS2). When information is

encrypted before it is sent to the cloud, the chance that usable sensitive information can be

intercepted and used is greatly mitigated. It is both the customer's and cloud provider's

responsibility to ensure that data is securely transferred.

Security Risks in Software Interfaces in Cloud Computing

Most cloud services are interacted with through software interfaces. Additionally, for

most users of the cloud who employ such a service for more than storage, this would be a

frequent activity. Activities ranging from management to monitoring are performed through such

application programming interfaces. This point of interaction presents another area of

vulnerability as far as security is concerned. Here, attempts to sidestep conventional data

management policy may emerge, accidentally or intentionally. Needless to say, the results of

having an insecure interface can be devastating. It may be as detrimental as a breach of an

organization's stored data and could also easily be as costly in the long-run.

Solutions to Security Risks in Software Interfaces in Cloud Computing

A customer must be vigilant in their hunt for a cloud computing service provider to avoid

using one which has insecure interfaces. Interfaces must be planned to prevent against policy

circumvention. To eschew running into issues regarding interfaces, cloud users should adamantly avoid cloud services which employ interfaces that use reusable passwords, reusable tokens, inflexible controls, unspecified access, improper monitoring, poor transmissions and improper authorizations. Moreover, users should themselves avoid contributing to any one of these precarious tools and practices.

An organization interested in taking advantage of the benefits of cloud computing but uncertain if the interfaces of cloud services are secure may find it helpful to form a nexus with a third-party investigator to find the IT processes of said organization a safe home. Research indicates that many small business, eager to get on the cloud but wary of the security factors, tentatively approach the cloud with the assistance of a third party whose job is to provide as much information about the functionality and security of the features different cloud computing services offer.

Security Risks in Data Storage in Cloud Computing

Once a system has been established to transfer information from local networks or devices securely, and interfaces are also made secure, it is then necessary for the information on the cloud to remain secure. Data storage is certainly the number one area of cloud computing security that seems to have many potential users concerned. No doubt this is the number one factor about cloud computing that makes CIOs, CTOs and individual users afraid of the cloud. When an organization or an individual has sensitive information stored in a local network or on a single device, the organization or individual not only has the luxury of monitoring very closely the different people that may access the information, they also have a much better opportunity to protect the information physically as well as through cyber efforts. In such a case, the organization or individual may employ physical monitoring systems such as cameras, physical security systems such as alarms, and computer-based monitoring and security systems as well. In short, the organization or individual has full control over the data.

In the case of cloud computing services, nevertheless, such luxuries are nowhere to be found. With the luxuries go the comfort and hence the popular uneasiness about using cloud computing. On the cloud, everything seems distant and uncontrollable. In some very real sense, this is the case. However, this feeling itself, is not a material threat. The three fundamental methods in which data stored on the cloud is actually threatened is through a malicious threat posed by insiders, a malicious threat posed by third party entities otherwise known as hackers, or an inadvertent action by the provider itself such as a glitch.

Insider Attacks

Very rarely does one consider that the service provider which they are trusting to provide them with whatever service they seek would have malicious intent. This is simply because it is rare. Nevertheless, it is not so rare that it should be ignored. In the realm of cloud computing, it is indeed a sad but solid reality that many service providers intentionally "hack-in" into their clients' accounts and rummage through sensitive material looking for opportunities for personal gains. With cloud computing is becoming more popular, and dozens and dozens of services starting up monthly, the chances of rouge cloud computing service providers increases. This nightmarish reality is further made possible by the fact that there have been no ubiquitously adopted codes for providing cloud computing services which limits those who can operate such a service or delineates under what circumstances such a service can operate. An active imagination is not needed to conceive of the damage that could be accomplished by such cyber thugs who only mascaraed as a business. Depending upon the appetite of the cybercriminal and the sensitivity of the material or the size of an organization which is unfortunate enough to be the victim, information as insignificant as names or information as potentially devastating as bank account data, can be illegally acquired.

No news stories as of yet has reported a case in which an entire cloud computing service was established solely for the purpose of maliciously accessing the information of the clients and using said information for the personal gain of the owners of the cloud computing service. Such an event, which would require a very meticulous and mischievous mind as well as a workforce of equal malevolence as the mastermind, would be rare indeed. What is much more likely, however, is that perfectly functional, pure-intentioned cloud computing service hires a cybercriminal as an employee. The cybercriminal may then, using his employment at the cloud computing company, access sensitive data of numerous clients. The threat of a cybercriminal gaining access to customer information and leaking it or otherwise using it for purposes not desired by the client is increased by three factors: lack of provider transparency, lack of provider workforce discipline, and lack of hiring strict provider standards.

External Hacker Attacks

Beyond the threat of a malicious insider accessing customer data, external hackers are a looming threat for data stored on the cloud. This is what is most feared by those who find that the benefits of cloud computing are far outweighed by the risks. Many dread the risk of hackers breaking into the system and leaking information or using it for other malicious purposes. Some cloud infrastructures are designed in such a manner that a hacker or group of hackers only needs to gain access to a single central control point to control the entire cloud server. This bold maneuver is known as "hyperjacking." In the even that a single hacker or hacker-group gained control of one cloud server which contained information from hundreds of different organizations, mayhem would ensue.

Considering the scenario from the point of few of the hackers may be a good idea in order to understand the problem. Hackers have different objectives for their hacking. Some hackers do it for personal gain, which includes selling information, gaining direct access to bank accounts, or establishing blackmailing scenarios. Other hackers cause mayhem as a means to exact revenge for something that an organization or an individual may have done to them. Another group of hackers still, engage in hacking for the pure thrill of it and enjoy being the cause of a catastrophe for their own entertainment. While the hackers that hack in order to exact revenge on an organization or an individual would be very specific as to who they attack, the hackers that do it for personal monetary profit and the hackers that do it for entertainment are not only unlikely not to care who the victims are, they are likely to want to have as many victims as possible in order to maximize their gain.

A cloud server, with all of the data that it holds, would be for these two groups of hackers, nothing short of a goldmine. A cloud server full of data from various organizations has essentially amalgamated a group of victims for the hackers looking to make a random and hard hit. Rather than have to hack into various separate networks in order to profit greatly or cause mayhem, the hackers that target cloud servers only need to gain executive access to the servers. In a way, such a cyber-infrastructure is a dream come true for advanced and dedicated hackers (Greene, 2011).

Talk of hackers infiltrating cloud servers is not merely hypothetical. Recent history is chockfull of such examples and their devastating consequences. The second largest data breach in US history was a breach in 2011 which victimized Sony Corporation's online entertainment services, Epsilon Data Management (Banham, 2012). The services were based on the cloud. While the breach resulted in no actual damage beyond downtime and no sensitive information was released, the fact that such an event could at all occur was very startling to the IT community at large and served as a confirmation for those wary of cloud computing.

The breach of Google's cloud-based email provider Gmail, which took place in the same year as the Sony incident, caused an even bigger stir in the IT community.

" 'Google had a big failure in March (2011), involving the deletion of 150,000 Gmail users' emails, applications, contact and calendar information-basically their entire accounts,' Mr. Heiser said. 'The email contents and contact contents were just gone. Google attributed this to a software upgrade that had unexpected consequences. It took Google four days to fully restore data to the impacted users, which is a very long time, given that Google characterized this as impacting much less than 1% of its accounts' " (Banham, 2012, p. 14).

The company has since reported that they believe that they are aware of the exact location of the origin of the breach, tracing it to China. Moreover, they claim to have uncovered the weak point in the application that permitted it. Knowing that even the internet giant Google can fall victim to such a breach has done little for the confidence organizations have in cloud computing in general.

A breach with a not so happy ending took place in 2011. The victim was Dropbox Inc., a cloud vendor specializing explicitly in cloud storage services. While not too much sensitive information was leaked, the company incurred "a class action lawsuit brought by users in July 2011 for failure to secure their private data and immediately notify them about a recent data breach" (Banham, 2012, p. 14). Apparently an "any password worked glitch" was at the center of the breach. Moreover, "plaintiffs alleged that Dropbox did not encrypt the personal data it stored according to industry best practices, according to reports" (14).

While GoGrid, a commercial cloud vendor, was not unlucky enough to be on the defense end of a class action lawsuit as Dropbox Inc. was, it was unlucky enough to be the victim of a breach which leaked more sensitive information. In March of 2011, the company was hit by a breach in which an unauthorized third party "possibly had viewed its customers' account information, including payment card data" (Banham, 2012, p. 14). The provider claims to have taken the immediate action necessary by notifying federal law enforcement authorities (14). "In a letter to customers, GoGrid stated that it believed the situation had been contained and that there was no indication that customers' personally identifiable information had been shared with unauthorized parties" (Banham, 2012, p. 14). Whether or not this is the absolute truth is certainly debatable. So far, no contradictory evidence has been brought to light.

Glitches in the System

The final way in which data on the cloud may be at risk is through inadvertent glitches. In such cases, because of an action or inaction of the provider, data is inadvertently leaded out. 95% of the time, this sort of disaster is caused by either inexperience or inattentiveness and therefore could have been avoided with the implementation of increased attention. The rest of the time, such disasters are unavoidable by any reasonable means and must simply be dealt with immediately and learned from for the purpose of strengthening the provider's cloud.

An example of this can be found in the case of the corporate giant Microsoft. The Microsoft Business Productivity Online Suite, designed exclusively for commercial enterprises was unexpectedly hit with a data breach in 2010 (Banham, 2012). Reportedly, in an awkward situation "Customers of [Microsoft Business Productivity Online Suite] cloud service apparently could download information on other customers of the suite, albeit inadvertently. The technology giant said it resolved the issue within two hours of its discovery, and only a few customers were involved, according to reports" (Banham, 2012, p. 14). Again, and quite fortunate for the customers and the company itself, little damage resulted from the breach.

Even with the examples of breaches mentioned above, comparatively speaking, it appears that cloud computing infrastructures and services receive far less breaches than isolated internal cyber data platforms. Considering the facts aforementioned regarding how cloud servers and companies that offer such services handle an immense amount of information about numerous organizations that is tantalizing to hackers, it should be a daily event that a cloud computing infrastructure is hacked. The famous fear many organizations have about sending their data and operations to the cloud and the fact that giants corporations such as Goggle have been affected by hacking in the cloud would seem to support this hypothesis even more. Why then, does it appear that the cloud is not hacked as often as all the variables suggest it should be? It is indeed a curious situation about which many theories have developed.

One group of IT specialist believe that the fears about cloud computing have been drastically overdrawn. They insist that the cloud is not as unsafe as its dissenters claim that it is and that various basic and advanced security features do a good job of protecting customer data. More specifically, they believe that those in the cloud business understand the damage a breach would mean for their business. Jay Heiser, who is the vice president of research at technology consultant Gartner Inc. is in this camp. He says "Cloud providers put more emphasis on security than other entities. If they didn't, they'd fall over" (Banham, 2012, p. 14). Heiser is not alone. David Black, chief information security officer at Aon eSolutions agrees. He says that "potential data breaches in the cloud are talked about a lot, but there hasn't been much to point to. The reality is that cloud vendors know that security is the big risk to their entire business model. If they were to experience a major breach, they're sure to go out of business" (14).

Another, group of IT experts hold a separate theory of why there appears to be so few cloud computing breaches compared to what is expected. Oddly enough this theory starts out in the same vein as the other one, but comes to a different conclusion. This group of people agree that cloud providers are very well aware of the fact that their security is essentially there product especially in a world where so many businesses and organizations are already wary of cloud computing. These theorists go on to say, however, that it is not avoiding a breach that the cloud providers are good at, it is suppressing the news of breaches that do occur. David Roath, risk assurance partner at Pricewaterhouse Coopers L.L.P. definitely falls into this school of thought. He says "their reputation depends on not incurring a breach; consequently, they will do everything they can, if there is a breach, to ensure it isn't made public" (Banham, 2012, p. 14).

Solutions to Security Risks in Data Storage in Cloud Computing

The solutions to security risks involved in data storage on the cloud can be divided into actions which customers ought to take and actions which providers should take. While cloud providers obviously take steps to ensure that their service is as safe as possible, experts recommend that consumers should also take on some responsibility and be mindful to ensure that they can trust their documents to their respective providers (Winterberg, 2012).

Insider Attacks

In order to mitigate the chance that an insider can lead to a data breach, customers should investigate as thoroughly as possible, the hiring processes and standards of the candidate cloud provider, the workforce structure, and the transparency provided. Customers should only consider using cloud providers that rate very high on all three frontiers.

Cloud providers can mitigate the amount of breaches that occur because of inside maliciousness by battening down on what the customers should look for: transparency, solid workforce structure, and strict hiring standards. Although they are improving with time, provider transparency for most cloud computing services has not been quite up to par. Often times, the customers are completely in the dark regarding how their information may be accessed, by whom it will be accessed, and under what circumstances it may be accessed.

In addition to a lack of transparency, weak workforce discipline and organizational structure of the cloud computing service providers also increase the possibility of a cybercriminal employee accessing customer data with malicious intentions. Cybercriminals abound and can exist inside a workforce (VanDerwerken, 2011). In the event that the workforce of a cloud computing service provider is not strictly designed and roles are not properly differentiated, there may come instances in which those who do not have access to client data are allowed access. A provider should have strict protocols outlining who has access to customer information and for what reasons they should be allowed. The stricter the workforce operations, the less likely an insider breach will occur. The less structured and differentiated the workforce of a provider is however, the more individuals will have access to sensitive client information, and therefore the more likely that a cybercriminal employee will eventually cause a data breach. "63% Of the 761 data breaches investigated in 2010 by the U.S. Secret Service and Verizon Communications Inc.'s forensics analysis unit occurred at companies with 100 or fewer employees" which are more likely to be newer companies and therefore more likely to lack in solid structure (Banham, 2012, p. 14). A large percentage of said breeches, therefore, are likely to have been accomplished with insider assistance.

Finally, having lax hiring standards can be devastating to a cloud computing service provider and more accurately, to the customers of the provider. In the goal to prevent a single malicious employee or even a group of employees from improperly making use of customer data, hiring is the first line of a defense for a provider. It is important that cloud computing service providers understand the gravity of their service. Some of the information entrusted to such providers could, in the wrong hands, potentially destroy the lives of thousands. Needless to say, the job should be taken extremely seriously. Many cloud computing service providers today hire with standards below that of Wal-Mart. This, many CTOs and CIOs agree, is unacceptable. Candidate employees must be scrutinized not only for their computer science knowledge and ability but also for their ethical standards. Some in information technology suggest standards so strict that they would have viable candidates as those who are completely free of any criminal charges even vehicle moving violations. While this may be a bit extreme, it is certainly important that only candidates who show absolutely no sign of criminal intent, past or present, be hired to work for cloud computing services, even if said candidate will hold a position that does not naturally allow him or her access to customer data.

Usually, establishing such rigorous hiring standards make it difficult to land the ideal employee. After all, not only would the company be seeking an employee that is knowledgeable in the field and reliable, they would also be seeking one that exhibits excellent ethical standards as well. Many otherwise marginally acceptable candidates may need to be rejected according to such standards. Of course rejecting so many candidates may naturally result in an understaffed workplace. To compensate for this, the companies would need to offer their employees a higher pay. This would attract a larger number of people which the company can sift through. The additional cost incurred should be passed on to the customers. It is ultimately for their sake that such strict hiring standards are being adopted in the first place. While it is of course impossible to guarantee that an individual hired does not secretly have malicious intent that may jeopardize the safety of client data, employing rigorous standards for hiring drastically decreases the chance.

External Hacker Attacks

To mitigate the chance that third party hackers will gain access to their data on a cloud, customers should seek cloud providers who employ intrusion detection capabilities as well as routine security checks such as audit trails. In addition to this, customers should seek cloud providers that explicitly take responsibility for the security for the information that they will hold. While it sounds, counterintuitive, many cloud providers do not explicitly own up to such responsibly. Additionally, customers should investigate diligently the background and history of all candidate cloud providers and make certain that there have been no serious security breach incidents experienced by the provider.

Cloud providers themselves must realize the importance of security to their customers. This realization should naturally lead to them to invest in resources that contribute to such security. The providers must provide state of the art encryption, advanced data-leak prevention, as well as regular content inspection. Moreover, they should be willing and able to reassure the customers by informing them in detail of the various measures they implement in order to ensure the security of their data on the cloud.

Glitches in the System

There is very little that a customer can do to predict or control the glitches in the system of a candidate cloud provider. However, as the best indicator of the future is the past, customers considering using the service of a cloud provider should investigate the provider's record and check for such glitches in the past. If the provider had a glitch in the past, it does not necessarily mean that they will have one in the future. In fact, it may have strengthened the company and even reduced the chance that such glitches will occur in the future. If a company has not had a glitch in their cloud in the past, it does not mean that they never will either. Customers, therefore, should pay attention to the company as a whole, investigating how many glitches, if any, they have had, how long it was since the last glitch and what kind of workforce and organizational structure is onboard to avoid such glitches in the future. An attentive company is the best one to trust.

A cloud provider knows little more than a cloud customer as to what glitches in the systems may occur in the future and lead to data breaches. Such events, by their very nature, are very difficult to predict. In any case, it is the responsibility of the cloud provider to continually review the infrastructure to mitigate the risk of such issues. Cloud providers should use as their guide, past glitches they have experienced, if any, the glitches of other cloud providers, and any areas of concern their IT personnel may report. The key to avoiding glitches which can lead to security breaches is remaining ever vigilant.

Conclusion

Cloud Computing continues to be a popular cyber topic and promises to continue to grow in popularity as the world dives into the second decade of the century. The commotion about the platform comes from its ability to greatly reduce operating costs for organizations and streamline IT functions. The benefits are outstanding and certainly palpable. However, equally as evident are the security risks. Holding back thousands of organizations is the fear that transferring their operations to a cloud-based system would leave them vulnerable to data loss and hackers. Even so, the reports of how many data breaches have occurred on cloud-based systems is much lower than expected.

Both cloud customers and cloud providers must have a solid understanding of the three most popular methods through which cloud computing is exposed to security risks: data transfer, interface interaction, and data storage. Moreover cloud-stored data is threatened by malicious insider threats, external hacker threats, and inadvertent internal glitches. They must be sure to understand that the each of these areas from which potential threats can emerge must be individually addressed. Malicious insider threats can be mitigated by doing as much as possible to make certain that ethical individuals are employed. The threat of a data breach as a result of external hackers can be mitigated by employing intrusion detection capabilities, audit trails, encryption, advanced data-leak prevention, and regular content inspection. Finally attentiveness and vigilance exercised by the cloud provider is the best prophylactic against an inadvertent glitch which may result in a security breach. Both customer and cloud providers have a responsibility to strive for optimal security. Customers should seek out excellent cloud providers and cloud providers should seek to be the excellent cloud providers customers seek. In the event that this occurs, cloud computing's advantages far outweigh its disadvantages.

19

References

Banham, R. (2012). Few data breaches in the cloud-for now. *Business Insurance, 46*(3), 14.

Greene, T. (2011). Cloud services useful for criminals. *Network World, 28*(2), 16.

Hempel, J. (2009). Salesforce hits its stride. *Fortune, 159*(4), 29-32.

Juels, A., & Opera, A. (2013). New approaches to security and availability for cloud

    data. *Communications Of The ACM, 56*(2), 64-73.

Langley, N. (2008). Google targets office space. *Computer Weekly,* 18.

Owens, D. (2010). Securing elasticity in the cloud. *Communications Of The ACM, 53*(6), 46-

    51.

Shacklett, M. (2011). Cloud computing. *World Trade: WT100, 24*(1), 16.

Tonellato, P. Fusaro, V. A., Patil, P., Gafni, E., & Wall, D. P. (2011). Biomedical cloud

    computing with Amazon web services. *Plos Computational Biology, 7*(8), 1-6.

VanDerwerken, J. (2011). Training on the cyber security frontlines. *T+D, 65*(6), 46.

Winterberg, B. (2012). How to stay safe when using the cloud. *Journal Of Financial

    Planning, 25*(7), 24-26.